The Anatomy of Solitude

The Anatomy of Solitude

Pitambar Naik

HAWAKAL

HAWAKAL

Published by Hawakal Publishers
185 Kali Temple Road, Nimta, Kolkata 700049
India

Email info@hawakal.com
Website www.hawakal.com

First edition June, 2019 (Paperback)

Copyright © Pitambar Naik 2019

Cover photography: Canva
Cover concept & design: Bitan Chakraborty

All rights reserved. No part of this publication may be reproduced or transmitted (other than for purposes of review/critique) in any form or by any means, electronic or mechanical, including photocopy, recording, or any information storage and retrieval system without prior permission in writing from the publisher or the copyright holder where applicable. The author asserts his moral right to be identified as the author of his work.

ISBN: 978-93-87883-68-0

Price: 300 INR | USD 8.99

for
my late father

Acknowledgements

As I shape this book into a reality I humbly recapitulate a handful of good people and publications which have truly instrumental in sculpting this collection of poetry. Their help in many ways kept my zeitgeist indefatigable.

I sincerely thank the editors and founders of a galaxy of international literary magazines which I regularly and on a daily basis read and sharpen the thought process. It's these magazines which indeed help me to be inventive.

I started writing in English back in 2013 and in this span of time my work snatched the pages of some finest magazines across 10 countries. The poems arrayed in this collection first found home in magazines like *Voice and Verse Poetry Magazine*, *Vayavya*, *Mad Swirl*, *The Literary Nest*, *Coldnoon International*, *Stag Hill Literary Journal*, *The Wagon Magazine*, *The Best Indian Poetry*, *The New Indian Express*, *Formercactus*, *Blue Lake Review* and *Spark Magazine*. I am indebted to them for their creative integrity.

My immense gratitude to my publisher, *Hawakal*, without their support this book wouldn't have come to life.

My readers, friends and some of the finest writers across the globe; though I'm unable to mention their names have unceasingly ignited and provoked me to script without a cease.

I am sincerely grateful to them. Last but not least, I have no words to express my heartfelt indebtedness to my wife, Bharati Mohanty, and son, Afresh Frankincense, for bearing with me and forgiving my aloofness and indifference at various points of times.

I hope *The Anatomy of Solitude* will be cherished by readers, worldwide.

Pitambar Naik
29th of May, 2019
Hyderabad, India

Contents

Agreement over a Cuppa of Cappuccino	11
The Coffee Table of our Duplex	12
They'd Meet again in Heaven	13
Tishani Doshi's Girls	14
Feminine Notes on the Hussain Sagar Lake	16
Diagram of a Torso	17
New Idioms	18
105 Degrees of Silence	19
Loggerhead	20
Lips, bones and Commotion	21
Prayer	23
Startled Periwinkle	25
Practicing the Love of Calligraphy of Galilee	26
Telegram of Folksongs	27
The Navel of the City's Loneliness	28
The Market is a Phial of Anaesthesia of Bourbon	29
Write to me to the C/o Address	30
Dilemma	31
First Kiss	32
You Belong to Virgo	33
Genealogy	35
The Armpit of the Mango Coppice	37
Mannequin	38
Coffin	39
Phoenix	41
Sick Eyes	42
The Anatomy of Solitude	43
Heartbeats	44
The Other Day I Watched a Pelican	45

Semicolon	46
The Bruised Lips of the Lilies	47
Elegies	48
Assurance	49
Sainthood	50
Solitude of Alabaster and a Thousand Other Sins	51
Savagery	52
Rancor	53
Bellybutton	54
The Blessedness of Christ was the Cosmetics	55
Pronoun	56
The Love Syllables for Valentines	57
Falling in Love with the Philippines	58
Nomenclature	60
The Beatitudes of Gethsemane	61
Hunger	62
Balm	63
I Can't Stop Drinking Your Shadow Songs	64
Love is a Lonely Territory	65
A Thousand Other Sins	66
Half Life	67
The Lent Season	68
The Love Affair	69
The Golconda Fort in Loneliness	70
How the Vintage Lives Merry-go-around	71
Aquarium	72
The Phonetics of my Boyhood	73
Our Blood Doesn't Look alike at Times of Riots	75
We Had a Passport to Melancholy	76
Solemnly, Dad Retires to His New Bedroom	78

Agreement over a Cuppa of Cappuccino

While patting your disturbed innocence you missed the last train
your anxiousness down the spine was hatching a conspiracy
did it smell a war disproportionately while revoking your hostility?
The evening wears a see-through, deep-black and low-neck couture.

For the whole fortnight, we're exiled on an island
the moonlight was silver love wrap in that café coffee of loss.

This is again a leap year; this is further a chilled winter
whereas ours is an agreement over a cuppa of cappuccino
I knew how your presence was the Dionysian warmth
that resembled the inside's righteousness of a penumbra.

Your body tilts towards exertion and recurring ache
I aggressively smell the workloads of your innocence
breaking the barbed giddiness insanely we sip rather intrigued peace
serving some slices of music, sandwiches with spoonfuls of aroma
you ask, how the bosom of laziness smells
how we get wilder around the hypothesis of ceramic saucers!

A tiresome middle-aged hypertension maybe hovers
a perennial ecstasy is the eulogy of your dry and pale skin
our first night's disheveled breathing was a memorial song
look, something beyond the mimicry
we come together for a facelift of our heartbeats
and just have the chilled condensation with creamy milk!

The Coffee Table of our Duplex

You do possess a lot of IQ on beauty but that's essential
why shouldn't you embellish the shadows around your eyes—
you say that's a camaraderie of hibiscus and your family ethos
the frame of transfiguration you wear is no atom of a dilemma
the intuition of physics creates a space of therapy.

The freshest spring descends surreptitiously as you yawn
over a cup of coffee at the time while soothing a scar of the millennia
we walked hand in hand to bury all conspiracies of metallic sorrow
our bodily paranoia was a season of respite with caffeine!

We thought to sweeten the conjugational longitude on the balcony
with the vapour concocted with nicotine and bougainvillea's orgasm
almost half of our surrogacy and its intimacy underneath was a locket
yours was sugar less and mine was little creamy and stirred up.

We clung to our ripe innocence to play with feverishness
and wished to be the mendicants of seductive hallucination
the coffee table of our duplex—a calling bell of connotation
often I take refuge peacefully in your lazy exertion!

Mother Said They'd Meet in Heaven

Father sat all day long to yawn like a *yogi* under the slab of loss
his mismatched past revolved around the Qumran findings
his eyes yearned from the thick lens of Cuba
to embrace mother's absentminded shadow.

He longed to recapitulate the reels of some unsettled accounts
and tried to exhume the coffin of his youthfulness in mother's body
forgetting all wrong calculations between mother and his fate
at dawn, the young siblings practiced Chinese *Kung-fu*
my absence perennially hunted them; mother was a summer's evening!

Sitting at the front porch mother smiled at the menageries of life
the backyard and the *sanyasa* of the old banyan tree was mystic
those loose-faced, hump-backed, saggy-faced folks
exhibited the architecture of their octogenarian gullibility.

May be a light dimly flickered in a lump of desert
a wayfarer there wound up the journey on the peninsular of smoke
a fisherman longed for a good catch of fate before the sun went off
mother couldn't figure out father's soft pneumatic etymology
only one thing she said, they'd meet again in heaven.

Tishani Doshi's Girls

The lipstick of the rainbow fades coyly in the mild rain
it's a minimalist's temperature in the scorching sun
are Tishani Doshi's girls openly, vibrantly, boldly, bravely
daringly, coming out of the woods in skirts?

Is freedom a state of mind in a screeching research hypothesis?
Some pub goers pee from the inside doors when on edge
but some young lovers exchange perfume canes and lingerie
with red roses, flying kisses and Wellington boots
they, Tishani Doshi's girls dare only at this hour.

They wish to be the remnants of the radicals carrying their coffins
why they are just treated or considered cheaper than an FMCG product
crashed under the inflation
or between the teeth of chauvinism or by the market economy
Sheila Rashid wishes to flutter the national flag
Gauri Lankesh fucked all smoothly sterilized myths and vulgarity.

Truly speaking freedom doesn't look even like a bottle of scotch

how Una smells of the fascist blood, isn't it an oxymoron of
shamelessness?
Some show their colour and that's very much hereditary of brutality
listen what goes at the fullest decibel in Lutyen's Delhi
poor Umar flees life, the constitution is a rough note now
cows become lovelier and divine
art is a whore, cinema a pair of bitches and religion is butchery
Tishani Doshi's girls screech from moving buses!

Feminine Note of the Hussain Sagar Lake

Stanzas of pity with the syntax of pulses yet remain insoluble
in the toxic marrow, fleshy rhythms make a feminine note—
a sad song though, the caged birds take a flight coyly
at *azaan* times or when church bell screams like Mary Magdalene.

A flowery tide—I reminisce how I made a wreath out of it
years back I and she slipped away like an ebb that's a fond memory
diving into the groins of the Hussain Sagar Lake is a sweet salvation
were we some newly married frolicking coots of origami?
The spring clandestinely travels to Egypt in a monosyllabic style!

A relation tickles in the wings of butterflies of neon and azure
you like star gazing and bird watching with sips of bear
I smoothly occasionally chugged and tapped your bare back
solitude is called the freshest full moon of octagon in your crescent
eyes!

A diamond pendant gazes like the hibiscus in severity
city folks aloofly inject intravenous into your body while you're as
sleep
leaving you like a malnourished mother
the Necklace Road twirls, swirls and stoops like a bleeding mermaid
stanzas of pity and the syntax of pulses yet remain insoluble!

The Diagram of a Torso

The branded grope of a face cream and blessing of a lipstick—
emit the strawberry essence of amnesia every weekend
you're a wearied spinster of storm and lilies
hang out for poetry on the edge of the Lumbini park
and swamp your anklets without manicure and *mehendi*
the black lines on the brows forget to mail the feelings
what is the diagram of a torso in the frames of mahogany?

Even at a time of loss once I caught your lips' vanilla isotope
in a reddish skirt and golden flip-flops you stood akimbo
to measure the size of your brassieres clandestinely
the history of your passion scented like night jasmine
or the fragrance of the Lord Supper of Sundays
I naughtily groped with your sleek uncovered look
your hobgoblin seeks the *nirvana* of eternity
the laughing Buddha there behind loses his concentration.

New Idioms

We peacefully wait for years on two various ends
over a cup of coffee to suck the essence and the eons
we eventually unveil the new idioms of peace and its womb
to hug the constellation of hot fountains in our inhalation!

Remember that reactionary paradoxes of meditation and *dhyna*
the assertive counterproductive duality
which pulsates with the gravitational force in the deep heart
and wraps the floods in androgenic poignancy
that comes by courier wrapped in a polyethylene parcel
the tepid and warmth veins soothe us with a pensive balm
you are clothed in the hues of periwinkles' perjury alone!

On the other end after a low pressure which makes us little shocked
I can't feel any magic in your absence I'm following your mimicry
an upsurge ensues in the blank pages of the Indus Valley!
you are again a chunk of fleshy plateau snugly live alone.

105 Degrees of Silence

For the past few years since our self renunciation
we team up for canoeing in grey clouds
as to foster heart full of anticipatory anxieties
in the middle we wish to retrieve the righteousness
the lost consanguinity of our exiled bodily warmth
of those Paleolithic molecules
a dip sigh merges in the ventricle of the chilling bones.

I feel otherwise and swim like a blind octopus
in 105 degrees of silence to slide out of your grip
with an anaconda's innocence
to temporarily make a home elsewhere
a handful of stardust floats in every fortnight
across the adolescent *mahua* plateau
down your poliomyelitis but let it strand lonely
desperately and haphazardly to resurge again with purity!

Loggerhead

Who does shout this doctrine of temperament?
those birds of chicken soup go free now
nevertheless the bliss of the holy hymns
they ooze from the groins of a lake
of the sweet valentine's moon
the street is at a loggerhead with time.

The clump of flesh of a race gulps abuses—
maderchod and *behenchod* is so common
some from the backyard blabber
about the gravitational force and horoscope
those humans commonly drink
the anathema of history, they tell them easily
your fathers know, your mothers know
their breasts and vaginas know etcetera.

Those people—innocent like balloons
suffer for the crime they never committed
a few loot the paradise but the majority
still live under the moon but in panicked pain
those rhythms' of the bones sizzle in hopelessness
the spirit of their breathing unceasingly at loggerhead
it's a different nomenclature!

Lips, bones and Commotion

You have reared a purple bipolar lagoon
    down your lips
    that circumnavigates
in a bucket of giggles
    like a
    traditional euphoria
    a nascent
    morning of Bastar
stretches its bones in commotion
    the pink
    ventilator violates
    the temperament
of a house gecko writes of history
    in the neighbourhood
    a gravity of
    absentmindedness tiptoes
    I haven't stopped
    rolling some ideas
    to and fro like an algorithm
    it's an Alexandrian anecdote
migrating to the farthest
    for a pitcher
    of coconut water
    to the land of

      honey, milk, spices and meat
      after departing from Egypt
      to live amidst
      the cedars of Lebanon
the wilderness doesn't matter.

Prayer

Does this road go to the apartment
of Chinmayee Sanyal?
May be we could talk later
let's mark the discussion with brackets
and the ending with a full stop of equilibrium.

Some bastard etymologies overlap
your love of Chinese minced pork
a roadside culvert heightens the blurriness
and all our apprehensions ping
the new season with 360 degrees
John and Peter didn't give us gold or silver
they offered prayer and we leaped at once.

We forget our discomfiture
in a watertight compact bond
permanently we hug monochromatic caesuras
across the park some look through their lenses
Mao's spirit—a huge dragon
the economics of inflation
—But, Marxism, any difference?

Jesus taught even more Marxism
a theology of giving

a theology of magnitude of healing
a theology of serving and beyond
before so many centuries!

Startled Periwinkles

Otherwise the market is in a little pinafore of chastity
you ubiquitously share some commonness
while sipping a lot of icy coffee and kidding with hot pizzas
your maximum aspirations wish to attend symposiums on
architecture
I ask the size and whether or not your waist has got elasticity
you dance *Bharatanatyam* but learn *taekwondo*
I say, let's go to a Chinese hotel to have mayonnaise
as to measure the bulging double excel torso from the biceps
the fibrous chocolate on your lips may be a vanilla-lashed titillation
if you want to be enticed, you have a reason
a flowery lingerie in the chartreuse winks at you
those bikinis are startled periwinkles just like bubble gums
or maybe a few pieces of Italian cake freshly arrived at Panaji
your anniversary is just a compromise of two hearts
your taste bud is adulterated hopelessly, I'm not panicked!

Practicing the Love of Calligraphy of Galilee

The candle drips its teary haemoglobin from its main vein
it's a season of similitude, similes and rain in Gethsemane
I don't use any metaphor to allude to the apostrophe
why is my love for pork and paganism not dear to that dialect?

Someone teaches about afterlife concocting with deprivation
and none raises their eyebrows; their thought is goose-bump
in the public gatherings in city
Vishnu Manchu talks food apps and *Hanuman Chalisha*
and mitigates the hunger of many through astrology, *lol*!

While practicing the love of calligraphy of Galilee
I look stained; you look stressed to explore an impression
with a bowl of soup with rose water and peppermint
we fast on the Lent season remembering the passion
but then we remain the same hyphen of asparagus
while searching for a new hope and life
we look at his sweating and bleeding at Gethsemane!

Telegram of Folksongs

The story of your past was a beach of water colours
with an estuary and edges of palm barricaded alongside
there someone's dream is strewn and scattered
and your long reserved family emotions grow like palm trees
hemmed in shells, conches and soothing breezes.

You had been happy with a relation of two dimensions
initially that was preserved in an anathema
of a different season and of an acrid recipe
amidst all your angst and misspellings; you looked cool.

The dispatched inland letters were absolutely a solace
the telegram of folksongs was a square size myth of the past
my childhood of course was a bibliography of pain
but altogether we conjugate the alphabet and rhymes of life

The Navel of the City's Loneliness

Dances are the old notes of the cool psyche and high pressure
may be the sexy costume of a Greco-Roman deity
that speaks an alien language with sweet syllables
this evening looks pale, shabby, confused and gloomy.

It's like the trauma of separation from a damsel's arms
or may be like a whole worn out drifted dream of my birth place
and exactly like the flowery myth of kisses
on the edge of the navel of the city's loneliness.

What upsets that warm weather in the quilt?
several doses of medications, several strokes of cigarettes
catch the humming aloofness—that's a hornet
several layers of antagonism stare at the squabbling paradox.

How can I be quick to vex a fury in the inglenook?
The city longs for its past portfolio in grey ash
who lets the igloo melt in the peak of a lonely obsequiousness?

The Market is a Phial of Anaesthesia of Bourbon

In a brown suede and Chinese bob you look so slim
you drive your posh *Skoda* to the market square weekly once
to purchase the shadow of your eyelashes
and pick up a few sachets of oats and cornflakes
a few translucent lingerie to heighten the endpoint
and *Lakme*'s sunscreen to bless your longevity.

You propound the market is little more than a graduate school
to practice algorithms, Pythagoras' theory and Confucianism
the market surface is a blackboard to draw the graphical antics
a place worthy to recall what is erased from your cerebrum.

You love to dissect the market on the chopping board
arraying the market economy on the dining table like vegetable salad
in the inverted commas
you say market is a phial of anesthesia of bourbon!

Preparing a logbook and monthly nomenclature of phenomenology
you bring the market to the edge of the living-room as well
as news of political antagonism and social decimeters
to hang it like the pendulum of benediction
and architecture of inflation mixed with a bit of emotion.

Write to me to the C/O Address

Her absence is glued with carbon nucleic acid; it's a desert of scorpions and centipedes. It stings and is almost macabre in the ovum and looks for the date palm's neurology! Her absence peeps like a cobras' tongue. Her last mail was a half glass of wine of the optimum potential; the last line in it was—if you like, you write to me to the c/o address. Her last dress was a pair of Panjabi *shalwar* and *kurtee* embroidered in Pakistani melancholy. Her absence is 2-liner poetry folded in the Telugu *langabunni* and *burrakatha*! Her absence may not be an incantation of astrology or an inscribed tablet of nudity of Ellora in the spam mail. At the end, a journey of thunderstorms yells and a flood of gratitude nicely makes a deal with pointillism. Her absence is an essence of the old pain and a city of bougainvillea's frustration. The body language of your lips and scent of your body remind me of her melancholy; this is just the tip of the iceberg—her absence!

Dilemma

We happily dreamt with glowworms in the tired ripe fields
and hoped for the new germination of swarms and bunches
after years of dilemma and the chilled gnome.

Though our arguments with the carnivorous
were invertebrate and we're disagreed
we haphazardly longed for the delicacy of cornflakes!

We're purposefully under the bondage of an old circa
of innocence, of anachronism and of poignancy
in stockpiles a deprivation lingers; others hardly notice that.

our heart-felt need was the inhalations of a dove's peace
for our bodily commitment under the sycamore tree
wasn't it the resolution of a facsimile living?

We designed an orchard of faith little organically
with dahlias and bricks to make the four walls of life.

First Kiss

There, things look little normal under a flat hullaballoo
drought, famine and cholera are old and someone's own
drawing a pulse of geography in Mumbaikar's accent
you dream what has never been dreamt of
the harvest season parties in a French bikini
the shores are little thirsty to swim with eels
a few clouds first time learn to kiss in thunderstorms
after an ordeal the deal at once became sensible
Delhi hides her face like a victim of acid-attack
in the back seat of an Ola car
a pastor's son watches porn
right after singing Hallelujah with the choir
there's another world of dilemma and diabetes
yet, it practices life probably through the flute
is that a cuckoo's nostalgia? You hardly believe it
at last the Italian rhapsodies of folk sacraments
look emancipatory in all sense, are you gullible?

You Belong to Virgo

With an age-old idiosyncrasy, I am chatting
astride the ceiling of a mystic conspiracy
it's hardly visible on the Google map
someone counts the silky gusto of raspberry's inside
I drape my hands around that pensiveness
down the old anecdotes of a summersault
a mystery looks tired like a parched bough of Myanmar
the longing of an isotope in the beating
of your heart takes a sabbatical
the spring attends the puberty in a cinematic way
hearing me?

You nod every time, in the Mesopotamian format
opining, that's called Valentine's formula?
Carrying with you a bit of Khajuraho's sensual perversion
that old derailed panacea needs to be rejigged.

All diagrams, pie charts, and asymmetric pointillism
look like the caesura of the maroon *mehindi*
this landscape sizzles in a cemetery like a stanza of eulogy
a titillating and abandoned sea strands as a rag picker
the aftermath of a quake—you belong to Virgo
I belong to some other
the tender syntaxes melt the mature proposal of the void

someone hitchhikes your old-fashioned business plans.

Hungry cranes of pale mist meditate down memory lane
those autumnal anxieties deceptively suck rain
and then take a flight to Jerusalem
it's that diagonal antagonism sneaks on us
at last, we canoe to a land of promises of butterflies
nevertheless an abnormal tinge
below the dark pillow of the past we throttle our pessimism
on the threshold of our mutuality a vintage aspiration
looks like a rainbow of depravity
we gather for an evening litany after years.

Genealogy

I've been writing this letter with crimson ink of Freud
since the Neanderthal Age from a fossilized cave on a canvas
It's my sincere endeavours to be sociable with elusiveness
boycotting a draconian trepidation of bonus
I'm here to shake hands with ashy darkness uncertainties
and share a room with an oasis-chanting.

Long, long ago I was a Sisyphus, before that a Phoenix
before that a melodrama with the *slokas* of mysticism
before that more or less *ahimsa* in Sanskrit
before that an interlocutor, before that a nomad
and much after that a great Romeo, this is my genealogy.

Down the centuries, I've been trying to explore a new human species
while leaving their footprints some of those old friends have hinted
I urge, come with me I'll show you their betrayal in vivacity
exposed in silk naked in an open museum
come with me and see how they spread peace of barbed fence
how they plant their teeth as landmines as an explosive slur
freezing their consanguine congeniality
I've been living, dying, living and dying like a chronic jinx.

We're not in a permanent world, I know
may be a flood will someday flood the Pacific

an earthquake may whimsically uncover the cleavage of the
                                             Himalayas
one day you'll certainly listen
that XYZ was an immortal Romeo, an imperishable legend
and you would throw a couple of thoughtful porcelain smiles
do you think it's something genetically developed or biologically
                                                    morphed?

I'm waiting for a fresh breed of dawn. It's not a monotonous
                                             monologue
I'm hopeful for a newer world to showcase the old love.

The Armpit of the Mango Coppice

In a patch of the sky down, life shyly lollygagged
a weaver bird yet dared the storms like Fukushima did recently
her fate deserted her as the Buddha did to his wife
puddles of ecstasy, sorrow of long jump
fun of marathon and *kabbadi* in the eucalyptus jungle
the tiny hope fought a silent war of phenomenology.

Sebati Sahu's childhood didn't witness a 4G era
in the loneliness and recurrence of absentia
a few dog-eared hieroglyphics, maps and a math box
and a tattered school bag were her beloved laboratory
the canons dreams were the gods of oxymorons
the expired Panasonic transistor would bring
the good tiding every day and she'd think of the glacier
the broken kite would get puzzled
there in the armpit of the mango coppice.

Mannequin

There's a tender spring in pink to sense the torso of sensitivity
the blondes in the vestibule are busy for a make up
some eclectic thirst haphazardly wafts in the maroon bushes
exactly the life-size desire of the adolescence smells a fire
and masquerade in the busy squares of different shapes
the ladies hostel nearby looks trendily curious like a casino
a glass of stirred up sepia brown wine is like *gori teri chunri* song
the parameter, radius, length and width of the breasts look to be
                                                                                     peace
try the size; touch the contours, wear the brink and gulp the taste
any damage in the groin? All is well in the exported park
a plateau spills its hormone with porcelain satisfaction
and breathes the essence and the glassy dandelions!

Coffin

Your backyard wears a lone painting of music
with a few pieces of pensive and teary *ghazals*
the lilies in the kohl lake ooze sad morphine
Picasso's brushes, jam-packed with subtlety
the Mediterranean Sea nauseates in ambiguity
since how long have you been quarantined?

Your make up box blooms the beauty of the Lady Gaga
to offer a few pegs of tequila though sensically
that's a flimsy grotesque; you left that time with no treaty
thenceforth the park, the street corners' coffee café
the nearest Malaysian massage parlour, all crawl in pain.

A surrogated river revives from a brief death
with a little cathartic infatuation
an antique life-size reverie heinously termite-bitten
swims across a silent hiatus down eternity
in the secret drawer where all those snippets gossip
I am heaping all my sins there, which can be safely locked.

In your absence, here I walk like a monk
in the lush pink bungalows, clubs, inns and bars
I've sizzling peace talks with those sweet enemies
you say peace is a sick mind's attitude

I wait for the new foliation of the old body
even the spring is hypocritical here
I tried to stop the time that carries my coffin now.

Phoenix

The sting of death never go oblivion, it smells like a curse
maybe no decipherable bitterness and deadly like a cobra's animosity
I'm forsaking the body daily like a diagram or a pie chart
it sways to and fro the icicle of the sub-consciousness
that old man's slow breathing resembles a faded canvas
I never get old to portray the enigma of my frustration
life isn't concocted with elixir of *pranayam* and mixed cocktail
as you open your eyes and stand invertebrate
why doesn't my body flicker to grey ash permanently?

The Anatomy of Solitude

A broken mirror shrouds its bare murdered body hesitantly
the seventh season's bridal makeup lurks in the drawing room
and your feminine silhouette thinks of horizontal meditation
in the farthest a thoughtfulness of mask clicks a photo
nights are like the Arabian folk music of life and longings
blended with the bliss and sins of jingle bells and the *ghumura*[*]
in the nearest metro station in normalcy or the body of dome
an LED display advertisement preens its face coyly
responding to your suggestive quaint eyes
rather it's good to munch a tin full of bliss with hot soup
look how I'm dissecting the anatomy of solitude in void!

---

*Ghumura: a clay pot musical instrument traditionally used by the people of Kalahandi in Odisha in India.

Sick Eyes

Between those thick obscure skies in city outskirts you explore a dog-eared dilemma; right with the advent of a medieval winter two smacked feelings chirp in your sub-consciousness. The cherries of Ephesus clandestinely look aromatic and godly to hug the early spring. The Himalayas become a very old metaphor that traveled sleeveless dabbing a lot of cosmetics with diamond and sapphire. What was the necessity to chide the chilled window panes and the bare cuss words? I smoothly suck your presence with precision in slicking winter rain with humming whisper; swaggering subtlety and stupefied tickling. The messages in the envelope of a diamond smile hitting the secret wound of a part of the sky. Furthermore, your fragile amnesia ruthlessly writes a mail. A whopping warm whirlpool dances around flooding nude kisses from the core to besiege my wildness. There's an intermittent honeyed-upsurge glued to pain, panacea and those entire sweet dichotomies. I hear the twang and grab the touches and the continental polyphony of your sick eyes.

Heartbeats

Under a sycamore tree, down memory lane years ago we erected a compartment of clouds with curly waves. Was that something called dry anxiety in the triangle? Was there any gap of cacophony or controversy in the square? We played cards and bit on scrambled eggs putting a star-studded roof chilled with tickling ventilation. By the cool breeze of the Coromandel Coast a flowery hope was drawn as cloth line; in the front we pleaded with our heartbeats to guard over us. Hear, this is not a story like a bougainvillea's pink or an enchanting incantation of *Malgudi Days*, hear a bit of astrological nuances in disguised trousseaus. Were we happy to search for our luck munching on the narratives of Newton's law and twirling prima facie of sunset on the Chandrabhaga beach? This morning the rest of our dreams got barbecued after a long chronic pain but still our heartbeats are constant!

The Other Day I Watched a Pelican

The other day I watched a pelican
preying on an Indian enigma in a hungry lake
a huge crowd carved on the pages of onomatopoeia
along the Sea of Galilee, a new heaven was budding.

In the evening that day, I was anxious
for different paraphernalia of different syllabi
of heart full of music, art and aesthetics of historicity.

I think my ten-year-old son is the next Picasso
his brushes play the mouth piano on canvas
his pensive eyes decipher the beatitudes of oceans' art
and all unrevealed etymology of filament and figment
embroidered by poignancy of sheer promises.

These days when I go to bed late night
I kiss a dream of a peculiar nomenclature of milk's white
that resembles the fecundity of Cleopatra's deception
and I meet the pelican blazing as a dim light
to celebrate the Passover-the festival of peace
while chanting the Archimedes' theory.

Semicolon

Is there no room for a second birth called saxophone?
Defuse the dystopia of a false history; if you can.

That island was trapped in a crocodile's bellybutton
in a watery petticoat, it screamed like Cherrapunji
later it's brought to the notice of an itinerary illusion.

A few strokes of cigarettes with a few hugs of the *atma*
and of course some pegs of betrayal was like a casino of kisses.

Someone's divinity in the bracket of slimness reverberates
the healing of chemotherapy reflects on a platter of broccoli.

The vacuum of bourbon may be little closer to me
else it pricks though like a familiar pain
that last time was a subterfuge I merged with a semicolon!

The Bruised Lips of the Lilies

Once while sitting for an agreement with silence
we both encountered the brutality of a seismic surety
quenching the thirst once every forty days like a camel's DNA
chopping up the restive breathing like a deceptive oasis
now we take all care to swath our injured void
and preserve our death in mummies
the anatomy of solitude dwelled indoors with a mystery
and after this we're in a different circa!

The worn out messages of the old mysticism has no teeth
when the time skins itself like a snake
to have a new incarnation we see a flowery deal
our memories bruise the lips of those lilies of cuss words
once before my rebirth and after my long sickness
at 2 am in the morning of September 27th in 2002
while meeting a triangular passivity in full inebriation
the last quarter of the deserted peninsular got
drowsily drowned like the fate of the Titanic
we keep waiting even today for the providence of agility
though we couldn't witness an anesthetic apocalypse
we meet life perennially fooling the truth of death.

Elegies

And I find an agnostic conscience sitting snugly with a whore
and somewhere the Pacific is a puddle to sail vignette dreams
a few stars fall off while night-surfing and lollygagging
a sky full of diamonds moisturizes that orphan plateau
a tiny deciduous crop field of green promiscuity
gets procrastinated overnight for no reason—tragic!

Lately the Bay of Bengal has started drifting off
when the moon takes a hiatus to get a body massage
you have tepid tears to have the holy communion
and you take a lot of time to chant hallelujah
a bunch of lesser gods pray in various syntaxes in full spirit
to release the masses of chained elegies and their grief!

Assurance

You walk past just throwing a smile of ceramic porosity
how does the ventricle pulsate with such syllables?
At the end of the day the assurance you dole out
melts like the evidence in September's horoscope
there're big brass cups, silver medals, and mementos
they clandestinely pray
wrapping their mouths with tissues mock at the morgue near by
certainly, that's enough to assess your accomplishments.

I was sunk neck-deep and was praying for an exodus
our plane had an emergency landing in the zero gravity
between the two junctions of cataract of Coromandel
there's no geography around us then
though you're an anxious idiom of solace and *bhakti*
I was coming out of a forest of pink and desert's trepidation
to reciprocate the gratitude and fetch the deluge of assurance!

Sainthood

I was sketching the other half of your heart on a canvas
with a million folk smiles of different trances.

A lawn of boulevards sucks the full moon in precision
in the Kama Sutra format
every fortnight for sure you mark the calendar of Panipath
opening the skin of history, am not I linking to your breathing?

In a season of war, bloodshed and in a landscape of hate
it's not necessary to touch your bosom of sainthood
so slowly, beat by beat and layer by layer quite prettily
you could look beyond the skin and its tidbits even!

The fossilised torso of a dream sometimes blossoms like your longevity
to catch dragonflies on the bank of a lake full of hyacinths and nitric acid
the tender mannequins of prosody live as paying guests
I rather taste this pain with a plate of *momo* and sausage
of the loss, of the compromise and of the pain of the millennium.

Solitude of Alabaster and a Thousand Other Sins

The notes of the Mandarin songs are like a sick mother's first
delivery
between two hemispheres of your absence
the scent of our first cohabitation spirals in the presence of a far-off
island
your departure is like a chronic tragedy of solitude.

Meanwhile, the aroma of Juhu beach is like a boyhood memory
I'm drinking the silhouette of our separation
with solitude of alabaster and a thousand other sins
after a bath with rose glycerin the earth menstruates red
I secretly wait to sneak on your departed divinity!

It's almost true; tears are a resemblance of the oysters in rose shells
and a few provoked urchin stars found decadent in your living room
the last day was full of parcels of whisper and farewell
of separation, of division, of seclusion and of the eternity.

Savagery

In the last week of August the Coromandel Coast froths
after a business discourse, our promises are so fresh now
it's around the waist of the northern peninsular we live in
a flight of ravens' suck the breasts of Machilipatnam
a hungry monologue stretches out its blank heart on the sea
in the last part of the year when peace fucks off war!

You got an offer to study Emily Dickinson, is she a metaphor?
A kind of feverish indulgence was a few pegs of champagne
a mystic whirlpool from a distant land smells of our passion
I couldn't concentrate on the abrupt abnormality?

Juliet laid her bulging love on Romeo's heart
in between us lingers a lucid Mesopotamian paradise
the freaks in us starve for unkempt propensity of love
with a hardcore craving for antiquity
we started smelling each other's savagery every day.

Rancor

You are leisurely walking across the addicted plateau of grey nemesis
the idiosyncratic suspicion interprets a shaft of divinity
your heart immersed in rain songs and folk music of an enigma
lately, I escaped an imported death at the crossroads of acupuncture.

The hottest market data of the time laughs at our closed-door affair
join me for a drink or two to construe a few economic subtleties
I am acquainted with your borrowed life now
that late night's anachronism after the deluge of drowsy mists
wishes to have a heart to heart talk
I've been habituated with those familiar dents, drought and distaste
these years are almost deciduous with no blessings.

The fresh meat and mushrooms in the kitchen fast look like a ravaged pain
they fear your aloofness and I fear your century-old rancor
your closeness, at last, seems to be a difficult conundrum.

Bellybutton

Those spicy dreams dangle like enticing pendants of a new season
a thirsty summer river smoldering for months gets back to life
your intimacy of turquoise gropes me; is it an ambiguity?

That old familiar song throws a smile from the top floor
it's little hallucinogenic like mild kisses of a nutritional supplement
may be the membranous strokes from your fatty lips.

I am hanging out on the verge of a ditch of deception
the wall clock above halts to take a glimpse of your bellybutton
a late drowsy winter afternoon is pregnant and lazy.

This terribly dry land goes wild again like a dessert's wrath
a fire mishap licks us in between our own monochromatic sorrows
we ceaselessly gnash our blood-stained teeth till midnight!

The Blessedness of Christ was the Cosmetics

In between us, we almost expect no epistemology
may be, this is the preamble of our constitution
sometimes an obsolete season takes a U-turn
along the thirsty coasts a consensual treaty bites our lips
a vagabond time suspects to agree with us
a vacuum seclusion lives in our bedroom as a trauma
on behalf of the ragged, tattered and worn out tears
often we helplessly longed to embrace our shortcoming
yet, you wear the blessedness of Christ as your cosmetics
and the cloth of our meekness eyed for a new birth!

Pronoun

Often even a dead body hugs mother Mary
with a letter of proximity written in the flesh of Hebrew
the spring in its jovial incarnation sits in lotus posture
yet, you are a divorced pronoun
you believe in the syntax of gyration
your new birth is a tapestry of apostrophes
these days you need a few pegs of the French tequila
before and after sex
to smoothen your living on a contract with hyphens!

The Love Syllables for Valentines

And I'm an ostracized idiom sailing on the Bay of Bengal
well, how can we allow us to be fringe fragments?
We're very much the reluctant fundamentalists
in the midnight even after the shipwreck
we both mutually try to get the dialysis of our blood
and tally our zodiac in a quilt of *Sheng-Fui*
the progesterone gland oozes a blissful serum
while listening to each other's heart on the roaring curvatures
I demystify the veiled appendix rooted in your aortas
season or off season you nurture a utopia of loyalty
and get ready to flourish the thin chastity of love syllables
year after year when the freshest longing become so deep
we withstand the fury of teeth, eyes and gnashing atrocity.

Falling in Love with the Philippines

I purchased an oil painting from a suburb of Manila
then you're already in the middle of your adulthood
you're already living separately with your Tunisian boyfriend
and we had had thickly substantive closeness
we're occasionally siphoning each other's sin—
while walking past the tickling secrets
we collided with the rosy porosity of many good things
to flip through the dictionary of metabolism
some seasons were empathetic with us afterwards.

We're a couple of yellow mollycoddling humours
in Banave rice fields, lost in hugging the proximity
when the enticing colours at *El Nido* induced us to draw our fate
we're soaking the virginity of the Chocolate Hills
however, our strategic marketing mix was standing apart.

We're unveiling all the veiled treachery of zinc and phosphate
the ensuing episode of those ups and downs were just the illusions
the course of your single motherhood was a snaky road
we drew an architectural diagram before we met in a prayer hall
after the sermon was over just before the benediction
it'd hardly been a few months after your separation.

Your eyes were just like the sizzling eccentricity of Queen of Katwe of bulging assurance of the next enlightenment

else may be more like a memoir of a few dollars
of a myth or that of the vague epilogue to the silent year of our exodus
the half breast of a Tibetan city wrapped in the Chinese indecency
Filipina, your company was the warmth of the shores of Batanga
—a prohibited but the most alluring body
the gracious nymphomaniac flora of Ceba
your dream wore the beads of the Boracay beach clothing in red fantasies
today, when I remember all this, you are just a sweet memory!

Nomenclature

A factory chimney fumes to swallow the sky alive; the bloody smell of a python's mouth under a solitary banyan tree hugs the tunnels we pass through. A summer fire burns in our eyes to lead us to sip some champagne gauging our heartbeats! History is not full of Queen Victoria's love affairs; the world of ours aptly hobnobs like immature adolescents erecting the antique desire—moon and lily's erotica! You wear a new brand of suspicion after the university timetable is out; I wonder whether or not that's exported from the Republic of China. One smells other's quintessential; the reflection of the cavernous hunger comes whining even in our absence. How do you name it? There's an ideology that lives in hate, war and acrimony; you nonsensically giggle with the moon's tepid behaviour.

The Beatitudes of Gethsemane

A pelican, as far as its devotion is concerned it looks quite otherwise
maybe not like a crow or a *kafir*, otherwise an adamant mongoose
let your emotion run clandestinely through the pages of the Song of
Solomon.

That write up on your asceticism and its fossil encryptions create a
record
people pick up this as a hot discussion of paranoia
when the sun rolls everywhere we love 100 degrees of seclusion
from the abyss of *dharma* you chant the beatitudes of Gethsemane!

The honey-suckers smell the bodily aroma of all tender spinsters in
the garden
it's a Valentine invitation, an inseparable longing of love
a diagram of insatiable acrophobia
it stings the ovum, the petals and furthermore the nirvana
it's a cheap offer in a beauty spa; like buy one and get one free!

Hunger

Tender ecstasy titters like a fairy tale as usual; still
an incarnadine hope takes a siesta in the mini heaven
ryes of milky hobgoblin scent and decay in the landscapes.

Here, listening to an mp3 of chirping chortles
in a star hotel in the heart of the city's soothing square dance
a fine lavish exchange of idyllic rendezvous
the east licks the hormonal love aubade of the west
while driving a ritzy future on, years go by
come on let's be megalomaniac, why not... why not
hugs of burgundy desires perennially embrace the present
French kisses and stings of honey love flood life.

But somewhere, you can't ignore a tattered diagram
a fierce storm in the air, bitter torture of crimson flames
see the parched ribs and warped stomach of Kalahandi
no harvest that year; kids in Phanus Punji's arms were for sale
a bit of stony mango seeds, dry mahua flowers
lips full of sweat, the brownish soil had no meaning
Bastar breathes hard to remain alive
Malkangiri is bitterly nude, Kandhamal sobs in the midnight
in an indifferent prism of trauma
the Bondas—Nature's pristine folks are just humorous sarcasm
numb hunger exposes its flint-teeth—
why is a huge exodus to death? Why is a spiraling screech?
abyss betrayal—a different *Bharatabarsha*
a bony world lurks width and breadth.

Balm

Remember the havoc in your thick apple red heart
your journey finishes in the middle of the rainy kisses
how to coin a new emotive reaction in the autumn season
your solitude is a bony whirlpool with disproportionate gravitation
the need of wrapping the name of the past can be realized.

A courier in a pensive parcel unravels the thirsty anxiety
you bring the tepid hope very close to your discretion
somehow we had a deal even with an earthquake
it erupts the old melic of solace and that's a healing touch.

May be a few drops of nectar from our forgotten story is a balm
—bear the magic of an upsurge: blessing and *moksha*
there's a constellation of a hot fountain that wears decadence
in the hot porcelain coffee cup the coffin of a lonely moon rests
what language does it speak?
It's the spring's love season on the balcony
which economic trick does it offer to sink with the world?

I Can't Stop Drinking Your Shadow Songs

You are clothed in *ghee* colour sensation of jazz
my childhood was a flowery plateau to snugly play with
this time I can't stop drinking your shadow songs.

Still I remember the gift you parceled form Santiago
on my 18th birthday missing the last letter of my name
and the 6th zero of the postal index numbers
many a time I remember the gnome and gorgeousness
how we engineered trains of matchboxes of contractions.

A factory chimney smudges the rosy lips of the sky
in a cloudy day with no electricity inside; it's like hatred
and the softest illusions allure the fragile apocalypse
the piece of land we live in hisses with heinousness
but, I can't stop drinking your shadow songs even in a fury!

Love is a Lonely Territory

It's tensed with a hyphen; the stardust of *mahua* plateau
home to your laughter; have you ever noted it?

Down your poliomyelitis, in the civil war era, my peace is a refugee
it strands desperately just as a few wingless waves.

Love is a lonely territory fenced by dots and garnished in brackets
the endocrine bliss of the holy hymns clot in your appendix.

The semi razzmatazz of a gloomy evening peeps as an enigma
frankly speaking that's a coffin of the bronze age
the creamy hymn on your lips
at bedtime the familiar rhapsodies ooze from Radha's Vrindavan.

Does peace wear the new costumes to sit across the table warmly?
Letting the kisses touch the tears of love and barbed fear
at last we ask each other to water our righteousness to blossom
around 300 kilometers now to go further the borders.

A Thousand Other Sins

Mesopotamia is a flat valley of hibernation with tulips
glasses of whisper and pints full of tequila gossip till late nights
a haphazard infatuation that encircles your solitude
the aftermath of the first pregnancy was an architecture
of peace, prima facie and pointillism
can you see heaven's thousand other sins?

We're some of the desiccated pronouns of the antiquity
and our integral self is outrageously eclipsed and fallen off
the creak of the mars' axis sends a telegram
when a war ceases our emotive speculation
it becomes the ceremony of half past 10
while frolicking with depression; the moon washes its semen stains
rain is a mirror of poetry and drumstick flowers
enough is the less of the rhythms of *rasarkeli*[*].

Often caesuras of our blood shells turn rectangle
gluing with syntaxes to drink a few more pegs of those other sins
the curve burns a camphor and smells the brevity of the vocabulary
however, smiles of this city germinate less camouflaged duplicity
depression is often a harmony of this part of the world
crowded intimacy is the new solitude of a joyful sabbatical.

*Rasarkeli is a word used to connote an ecstatic love affair in Sambalpuri folk songs in Odisha.

Half Life

The brief hiatus of your salvation
paints an acrylic garden of skins, veins and pulses
you stir a glass of milk like the storm of sins
when summer is around the corner
you cheer to a mug of palm juice
after a nice meal, the chronic complaint
is your invertebrate pain
why you don't forget to reminisce
how shy you were
after the first HCG and BCG tests
those syllables intentionally slipped to your midriff
you winked like polyphonic poetry of Gulzar
this afternoon's mail is a great solace
to eliminate any disaster in between us
yet you feel it's an epitaph of a half life!

The Late Lent Season

After the hurricane our panicked forgetfulness flicks us together under a roof of vinegar. We rise like a whirlpool in the guise of parachutes; the grey dawn sends a message through a magpie's voice. The gap of your closed heart is a solo *raga* and you breathe via its cleavage! The gullible evening breeze is decrepitly taciturn to grin the humid sunshine. We enter the solar eclipse of *tretaya yuga* sweetly. Is that a communication error? Those questions sweetly interact with the antiquity in the cave of your laughter. The icicle of those frictions throw a slant eye, when you go into depression in the lent season; the residue of your worn out fate curls to blossom with a heavy panache of filigree; and I ask, is it a nonchemical isotope copying our history and body language?

The Love Affair

Between two rivers of smoke
a rebellious canon squabbled
there's a wild fury alive named
Gauri Lankesh*
the ripple of truth was never a myth
that defeated the centurions of rancor
the untidy angst snugly yawned
brushing off the death of hydrogen.

You gazed at town folks—
were you a Phoenix?
The happiest quantum of life had to prove
the sheath of Oedipus wrong
in the thronging longitude of hate
the pure unmixed inhalation stopped
two bullets were like Hitler's venom
for chocking the love affair
with god, divinity, souls and soil!

*Gauri Lankesh was a journalist and shot dead in Bengaluru by right wing fanatics in Sept 5th 2017.

The Golconda Fort in Loneliness

The mirage of history nauseates
like an old man's wrinkles
in the city suburb a desiccated culvert grimaces
the yawn of a chronic pain
looks just as a doppelganger of retirement
that peeps through the fissures of angst
in panic, loneliness of asymmetrical palindromes.

Tombs, tablets, and inscriptions of elegance—
that's a tattered body
whispers on the street in acrid pain
the half-rotten assurance, yet a wasp of goodness
in the lanes beside a valetudinarian smile.

The last touch of pride is the residue of folklores
the lost clip-clops of horses and daggers
and war bugle look so meek this time around
that might be just a museum of the blitzkriegs
or a silent morgue in the cesspool of loneliness
the elegies of *Eid-ul-Fitr*—
splash the high of exuberance
layers of pain and palindromes
resemble the song of the Golconda Fort!

How the Vintage Lives Merry-Go-Around
For Dashrath Majhi

Disturbed but relentless, the blood was radioactive
the ribs were like dry *peepal* leaves
the saga of two decades and plus
made him an avenger
a peaceful storm that gaily sweated to kiss
wife's death and the god inside her womb
the bulwark was to sing a love song heliocentric
the grouse of the mountain melted
the pulses sawed the adamant pride
which species was the chunk of the soul?
Which breed was the shaft of the body?

Believe, a shard of heart was love-hit in Bihar
the tendon in the forearms and knuckles
could tilt the sky like another Hercules
the spine was hit harder yet the war was flat
it bloomed twenty-two times altogether
the makeshift spirit stopped to hit the shovel
on an epitaph, on a tomb of sacrifice
look how the vintage lives merry-go-around!

Dashrath Majhi known as the mountain man; who invested 22 years to break a mountain to lay a road for thousands in Bihar!

Aquarium

And for quite sometimes you loved to play golf in gestation
how can I forget your pencil sketch of surrogacy?
Dad's second stroke and the ensuing ruthlessness
was a huge setback for us down the decades
Mom's drifting into a prayer room to bless Dad's soul
was quite normal for years.

Clashing with a joie de vivre may be of different ilk
but I'm sure something shrinks in between the two selves
it's for the last time in history; you never look like the pathos of
strawberry
I note the whole story of ours in precision after we're fatally
detached
and struggled to survive ruthlessly in the pain of an aquarium!

Autumn takes a couple of dance lessons in the curvatures of nudity
in the middle of the sea the alchemy of neutrality agitates
you alleged me for having taken revenge on a treacherous time
night's thin gaudiness augments greedily in silence without our
consent
your deep amatory desire was a corrugated lake.

I walk back home taking your sea of pain in a creel to draw a map
the safe heaven which you've trapped for quite sometimes escapes
we've bifurcated that eternally by a barbed semicolon
those maroon promises get suffocated in a trap
and we hardly take notice of ourselves in the crowded cafe of
solitude

The Phonetics of my Boyhood

Mother taught me the phonetics of hoxagonal topology
and the prosody of serene phoneme
with the pulse of sensibility
she made me memorise the tables
of a banyan tree's innocence oftentimes
promising a reward for every answer
she helped me practice the formulae
asking to surf the galaxy of truth alongside
even pain might be your apple-red beloved
of your heart, she reiterated.

I accompanied her to the park and cinema;
like a ghost in her sari drape or a shadow in precision
of course, I wasn't a boy with less IQ
she drove as usual very grave to reprimand
some of the gods of small things
in the market she would sip a cup of cinnamon tea
with Udupi *uttapam;* when I said that I loved the *Lee* brand
and *Reebok*'s tawdriness
mother would gift just a cowboy's hat
and a pair of South Korean T-shirts
or hardly some mediocre goggles
the *Nivia* store always remained an illusion.

Mother was obviously not poor at mathematics
but exceptionally good
even at the theory of diminishing marginal utility
she fumigated the seeds of economic conundrums
coinciding the art of pole-vaulting
and the nuances of Newton's formulae with it.

Often she chased me to dare skydiving like eagles
and snow surfing like penguins
she sounded the phonetics—pain might either be the replica
of Abraham Lincoln's laughter
or an antique love letter of Cleopatra
otherwise, the joy of Uncle Tom's redemption!

Our Blood Doesn't Look alike at Times of Riots

What is the body language of the encroached border between us?
It wears a lollygagging ornament in spring
and preaches a sermon of pancreas
to provoke us seasonally half circle, it watches like the conscience
the surnames of their bones cry foul
as usual, our blood doesn't look alike at times of riots
lives over-layered with a kind of oration rather than shalom
the butchered manhood there looks for a sestet or aubade of love
why we see each other's forehead to find the difference
and crawl like earthworms of acrophobia
we barter everything accumulated for eons to cocoon ourselves
their clan, our clan, their faith and our faith and so on
we erect minarets several times higher than our loss
and then we christen it hate rather than roses for each other
then permanently fossilize our unrevealed selves layer by layer.

We had a Passport to Melancholy

In the belly of a strange tulips garden
the smell of a green pasture breathed olive
does magnetism connote uncertainties
can peace be garnished only after war?
Does homeland become an illusion?
There's ample flavour of mint leaves
Poiegrass, mushroom soup and other salvation
astonishingly our gloomy tears canoed across 7 seas!

We lived a life ambivalently, we wore the assimilation
of harp and saxophone's ambiguity
we fulfilled all deficits and got accustomed to
the prescribed way of life
though dancing to their pop was our weakness.

While sipping coffee on the balcony
we blamed on flawed foreign policy
while standing in the queue at the public store
we blamed on our fateful migration
while sleeping with phobia
we hatched the plan of escaping the extradition!

Being from a distant land is like
being children of a crisis of mayflies

our language couldn't speak the pulse of the land
and we're like expletives of shame
and dead bodies of nightmares
on the edge of racial cauldron and chagrin hit
immigration was no more the chestnuts of a panacea!

Hurriedly from an hideout of helter-skelter
we rushed to escape our bodies and unproved illegalities
behind those murky fences we buried our dreams
and baggage of predicaments
what was left to figure out?
The water fronts, the pain of departure
we had a passport to melancholy!

Solemnly, Dad Retires to His New Bedroom

Mom's solitude becomes an antiquarian shadow, lately
a deserted onomatopoeia accompanies her round the clock
she asks her drowsy sighs for a chance to go further
the winter sky sketches an obituary of silvery tears
dad retires to his new bedroom solemnly
making mom's absence his pillow with soft care
in the sepulcher, in sepia dark, in eternity
in the absence of packed solitariness
may be his body accepts a new world of hope
mom prays now and crosses over the Red Sea.

www.ingramcontent.com/pod-product-compliance
Lightning Source LLC
Chambersburg PA
CBHW031458040426
42444CB00007B/1144